D1254982

THE
JEWISH CHILD'S
BOOK OF
SPORTS HEROES

THE
JEWISH CHILD'S
BOOK OF
SPORTS HEROES

by
Robert Slater

JD | **Jonathan David Publishers, Inc.**
Middle Village, New York 11379

THE JEWISH CHILD'S BOOK OF
SPORTS HEROES

by

Robert Slater

Copyright ©1993

No part of this book may be reproduced in any form without the prior written consent of the publisher. Address all inquiries to:

Jonathan David Publishers, Inc.
68-22 Eliot Avenue
Middle Village, NY 11379

Library of Congress Cataloging-in-Publication Data

Slater, Robert, 1943–
  The Jewish child's book of sports heroes/by Robert Slater.
    p. cm.
  Includes index.
  ISBN 0-8246-0360-5
  1. Jewish athletes—Biography—Juvenile literature. I. Title.
GV697 .A1S54 1993
796' .0922—dc20
[B]   92-40087
                                                  CIP
                                                   AC

Book design by Jennifer Vignone
Printed in Mexico

TABLE OF CONTENTS

INTRODUCTION

Every time Sid Gordon, the great National Leaguer of the 1940s and 1950s, came to bat, my grandfather reminded me that "Gordon is Jewish." I never had the nerve to ask my grandfather what Sid's religious heritage had to do with his "socking" the ball out of the stadium. I cared only about how many home runs Gordon hit that season. But my grandfather's wonderful obsession about Sid Gordon's Jewishness started me in search of Jewish sports heroes.

It has become widely accepted that few Jews have had impressive sports careers. That is hardly surprising. In the olden days sports were believed to go hand in hand with pagan worship. That distaste for sports carried through to modern times. The parents of many of the sports stars in *The Jewish Child's Book of Sports Heroes* often placed little value on sports. They wanted their son or daughter to be a doctor or a lawyer, not a ball player.

The trouble was that sometimes their son or daughter preferred the gym or the playing field, and discovered that he or she could be as good, if not better, than the non-Jews engaged in a favorite sport. Often these "rebels" from traditional Jewish values found great success in the sports world.

Some of these Jewish sports stars have become quite famous and are included in these pages. There is not only Mark Spitz, the Olympic swimmer who won seven gold medals at the 1972 Munich Olympics, but also Sandy Koufax, the gutsy left-handed pitcher for the Brooklyn/Los Angeles Dodgers; and Harold Abrahams, the British track star at the 1924 Olympics, who was known mostly to track enthusiasts until the appearance of the 1981 movie *Chariots of Fire* which recounted his story. There are also bullfighter Sidney Franklin and some top-flight tennis players who are still competing: Brad Gilbert, the best Jewish tennis player of the early 1990s, as well as Aaron Krickstein and Amos Mansdorf.

Indeed, as you will discover in this book, Jews have been doing quite well in the sports world going back to the nineteenth century. Now, for your entertainment, I want to present thirty-one of the most talented Jewish sports heroes of all times.

Robert Slater
Jerusalem, Israel
March 1993

Harold Abrahams
The Chariot of Fire

Harold Abrahams, who was the subject of a major movie, *Chariots of Fire* in 1981, was one of the greatest sprinters in English track history.

Harold came from a wealthy, athletic family. He was born in 1899 in Bedford, England, and, encouraged by his elder brothers, began running at eight years of age. He won his first 100-yard race at age 12 with a time of 14.0 seconds.

From 1920 to 1923 he was a law student at Cambridge University where he became one of the school's greatest track athletes. But at the 1920 Olympics in Antwerp, Belgium, he was not among the winners in either the 100-meter dash or the long jump. As a result, he decided to concentrate only on sprinting.

Doing well at sprinting, Harold believed, was a way to fight back against those who disliked him because he was a Jew. To improve his chances at the 1924 Olympics in Paris, Abrahams hired the best sprinting coach in Britain, Sam Mussabini, who was half-Arab and half-French. Harold prepared to compete in the 100-meter dash.

His intense training with his new coach paid off even before the Olympics. On June 7, 1924, a month before Paris, Harold Abrahams set the English long-jump record of 7.38 meters (24 feet, 2$\frac{1}{2}$ inches), a record that stood for the next 32 years.

After Harold's long jump achievement, the British Olympic organizers decided that Harold should compete not only in the 100 meters, 200 meters, and relay races, but also in the long jump at the Paris Olympics. Abrahams wrote an anonymous letter to the *Daily Express*, arguing that he should not be expected to participate in the long jump and run the 200 meters since both events were to take place on the same afternoon. The letter was effective: Harold was excused from the long jumping.

Abrahams' greatest moment as a track star came on July 6, 1924 when he won the 100-meter finals at the Olympics. He was the first European to win an Olympic sprint title and also the first and only Briton to capture such a title. He considered his victory not only a triumph for Britain, but also an appropriate answer to the anti-Semitism that he had experienced.

In 1925 his career ended when he broke his leg. He became an athletic administrator as well as a sportswriter. From 1925 to 1967 he was athletics correspondent for the *Sunday Times*.

Harold is a member of the Jewish Sports Hall of Fame in Israel. Harold Abrahams died in 1978.

Jewish Sports Hall of Fame

1924 Olympics. Harold Abrahams, winner of the 100-meter dash.

Amy Alcott

Her Backyard Became a Miniature Golf Course

Born in Kansas City, Missouri, in 1956, Amy Alcott is one of the top women golfers, winning 29 golf tournaments, one short of the total needed for automatic entry into the Women's Golf Hall of Fame.

Amy grew up in Santa Monica, California. She loved watching television on Saturdays with a bowl of ice cream in her hands. Amy was a tomboy and from the time she was nine years old she hoped to become a professional golfer—even though she thought only men played the sport.

She began taking golf lessons as a child. Amy practiced hitting golf balls into a net and studied her swing in front of a mirror in order to improve it. She turned her backyard into a miniature golf course, hitting balls six hours a day.

Amy cut the grass short enough so she could putt, and she put soup cans in the ground for cups. She chipped over the hedges to the cups. "I dropped balls eight feet from the cup and would say to myself, 'This putt is for the Open Championship.' You'd be surprised how many I made."

Amy put her entire life into her golf game, feeling guilty when she did not practice. "I can remember watching TV back when I was still a kid and thinking I should be outside chipping about 1,000 balls."

Freckle-faced, brown-haired, possessing strong arms and a powerful body, Amy Alcott won the Junior Girls title at the age of 17 in 1973. Two years later, she won her first professional tournament at the Orange Blossom Classic. It was only the third tournament in which she had participated, a feat not equalled by any other woman pro golfer. She scored a record nine-under-par 207 (68-68-71), and received a $5,000 check for her victory.

Amy won 12 tournaments in 1980 and was named *Golf* magazine's Player of the Year. She enjoyed her greatest success in 1988 when she won the first major tournament of the year, the Nabisco Dinah Shore, and fifteen more. She finished the year among the top ten golfers. Her tour average was 71.71 strokes. For 1988 her total earnings were $292,349.

What is the secret of her success? Amy suggests that it is "learning to keep yourself totally under control," and never to think of yourself as a loser.

Amy Alcott

Praying for a birdie: Amy Alcott, golf star of the 1980s, zeroes in on the hole.

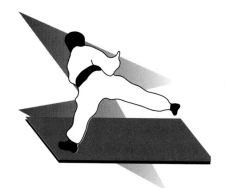

Yael Arad

First Israeli to Win an Olympic Medal

Yael Arad admits that people thought she was crazy when she took up judo at the age of eight. Boys who were not used to seeing girls pushing, shoving, and fighting, challenged her to fights.

"They weren't used to seeing muscular women," Yael laughed. "But look at me, I hardly look like a gorilla." Yael was born in Tel Aviv in 1967 and became an expert in judo because of her older brothers' interest in the sport.

Fast and strong, she is quite capable of pulling an opponent off her feet at a second's notice. "There's nothing more enjoyable than to throw another child down," says Yael with a grin.

When she was nine years old Yael took "only" second place in an Israeli judo championship. She was devastated. "I cried for three straight days and wouldn't leave home," she said. A year later, however, at age ten, she became Israeli judo champion in the 31-kilogram (68.2 pounds) weight class. She kept the title for six years.

In 1985, when Yael Arad entered the Israeli army at age 18, she did not have time for judo. Her job in uniform was sports instructor. Two years later when she was released from the army she faced a crisis. All her friends planned trips abroad to have fun, and if she wanted to become a world-class judoka, she would have to stay at home. On top of that, she lacked the money to train properly to compete in international competition.

Finally the Israeli sports authorities agreed to support Yael and her career blossomed. She placed third in the 61-kilogram (134 pound) division at the World Championships at Barcelona in July 1991.

Early in 1992, she captured a gold medal in the women's 61-kilogram division at the Paris tournament. For

Yael the most exciting part was hearing *Hatikva*, Israel's national anthem, play while Israel's flag was waving above.

In the spring of 1992, as she prepared for the Summer Olympics in Barcelona, Yael was named Israel's best athlete of the year. Her dream "to be the best in the world" in judo almost came true on July 30, 1992. In Barcelona, she placed second and captured the silver. She was the first Israeli ever to win an Olympic medal.

Yael lives in Herzylia, north of Tel Aviv with her parents, both of whom are journalists.

Israel Government Press Office

Yael Arad (right) and her mother, Nurit, upon Yael's return from capturing the first Israel Olympic medal ever at the 1992 Barcelona Olympics.

Arnold "Red" Auerbach
Basketball Coach Numero Uno

Thanks to Arnold "Red" Auerbach, their coach, the Boston Celtics dominated the National Basketball Association (NBA) in the 1950s and 1960s.

Always colorful and controversial, "Red" yelled at referees for making bad calls, imposed strict discipline on his players, and always showed up for a game puffing on a big cigar.

"Red" Auerbach was born in Brooklyn, New York, in 1917. He was a star basketball player in his Brooklyn high school, and later at George Washington University. After graduating from college he became a basketball coach.

In 1946 he was the first coach of the Washington Capitals, a pro basketball club that won 115 games and lost 53 in three seasons.

He became the Celtic coach in April 1950, taking over a team that had finished last in the Eastern Division of the NBA the previous season. Between 1950 and 1966, he was the most successful coach in basketball history.

The Celtics finished second in the Eastern Division four times between 1950 and 1956. Then, in the 1956-57 season, with center Bill Russell giving the team great defensive power, the Celtics won their first NBA title. However, in the next season the Celtics lost to St. Louis in the championship final.

After rebuilding the team around Russell, Bob Cousy, Bill Sharman, Frank Ramsey, Tom Heinsohn, John Havlicek, and the Jones boys—K.C. and Sam—Auerbach took the team on a winning spree unprecedented in NBA history. From 1959 to 1966, the Celtics won the league title eight straight times. Auerbach's overall coaching record of 1,037-548 is the best ever achieved by an NBA coach.

Coach Auerbach insisted that the Celtic players play team basketball and not try to be individual stars.

Auerbach's coaching techniques included fining players for every minute they were late for practice. He had good instincts and knew when it was wise to substitute one player for another.

In 1964 Auerbach became vice president and general manager of the Celtics. The following year he was named NBA Coach of the Year for the first time.

In 1966 "Red" retired from coaching but stayed with the Celtics, first as vice president and later (from 1971 on) as president.

In 1968 "Red" was inducted into the Basketball Hall of Fame. He is also a member of the Jewish Sports Hall of Fame in Israel.

Boston Celtics

No one coached an NBA team better: "Red" Auerbach, the long-time coach of the Boston Celtics.

Angela Buxton

Only Jewish Woman to Win a Wimbledon Title

Angela Buxton, one of the greatest woman tennis players of all time, was born in Liverpool, England, in 1934.

In 1940, during World War II, together with her mother and brother she was evacuated from England to South Africa. Her father remained behind.

Angela began playing tennis at age eight while attending a convent school in Johannesburg. She practiced every day on the convent's tennis courts, and was instructed by a visiting coach.

When she returned to England in 1946 at age 12, Angela realized that she was a far better player than her contemporaries who, because of the war, had missed out on tennis altogether.

When her parents' divorced, Angela moved with her mother to Llandudno, North Wales, where her mother's parents were living.

At school, opportunities to play tennis barely existed for Angela. Tennis lessons were given to a few select pupils, and Angela was given lessons that lasted only a half-hour per week.

Recognizing Angela's potential, her tennis instructor advised Angela's parents to enter her in tournaments. Mrs. Buxton asked if he meant Wimbledon. The instructor laughed and suggested starting with lesser tournaments.

Although her father knew so little about tennis that he could not even keep score of a tennis match, he offered to finance Angela's tennis career. He began by helping Angela and her mother move to London in 1950. In London she studied for one year at the Polytechnic, specializing in domestic science. In the meantime she kept working at her game.

To improve even more, Angela moved to California for six months, where she was coached by Bill Tilden, the great American star. Returning to England, she fared poorly and considered quitting the game. But in 1953, she won two gold medals at the Maccabiah Games in Israel. This established her as a genuine tennis star.

By 1954 Angela was ranked No. 4 in England, but her best season came two years later, in 1956, when she won the English Indoor and Grass championships as well as the hardcourt doubles title (with Darlene Hard). In 1956, she also won the doubles (with Althea Gibson) in both the Wimbledon and the French Open. Her crowning achievement was reaching the singles final at Wimbledon that year, only to lose to the American Shirley Fry.

Angela's great tennis career suddenly came to an end in 1956 when she hurt her wrist. She then opened the Angela Buxton Center, a tennis school in London's Hampstead section.

Today, Angela Buxton devotes her time to writing and lecturing about the tennis scene.

Angela Buxton

Angela Buxton, the 1956 Wimbledon Doubles Champion, poses at the net.

Howard Cosell
A Very Unusual Sportscaster

Howard Cosell, born Howard William Cohen in Winston-Salem, North Carolina, on March 25, 1918, grew up in Brooklyn, New York. His parents, Isidore and Nellie Cohen, were immigrants from Europe. Howard's father became an accountant for a chain of clothing stores.

Although Howard wanted to be a newspaper reporter, his parents convinced him to enter law school. He graduated from New York University in 1940 and began to practice law. One year later, in December 1941, he enlisted as a private in the U.S. Army.

Discharged from the army in 1946, Howard spent the next eight years as an attorney. In 1953, an ABC program manager asked him to assemble a panel of youngsters who would interview athletes for a weekly series of coast-to-coast radio programs. Howard was asked to serve as moderator as well. He jumped at the chance. One panelist was future broadcaster Marv Albert.

Three years later, in 1956, ABC offered Cosell $250.00 to do ten five-minute sports broadcasts. The programs were a success, and from that time on Howard gave up law practice and devoted all of his time to broadcasting.

Cosell's fame grew more widespread when he gave vocal support to the controversial heavyweight boxer Cassius Clay. Not everyone took Clay seriously when he turned Muslim and changed his name to Muhammed Ali. Cosell did. That angered Cosell's more conservative audience, but it did help Ali gain the needed respect.

Howard Cosell revolutionized sports broadcasting. Before he came along, sports announcers provided the play-by-play only, without analyzing the players or the issues. Cosell, however, cared deeply about what the players thought. He was often brash, even insolent, asking sharp questions at news conferences.

Over the air, Cosell delivered a wide variety of opinions. He lashed out at the boxing world for being brutal and corrupt. He assailed colleges for cheating and for academic abuse. He argued that the Olympics had become commercialized. Yet, Cosell was sensitive. He refused, for instance, to give out ball scores the day after Robert F. Kennedy was assassinated in June 1968.

In 1970, Howard Cosell became the outspoken commentator on ABC-TV's "Monday Night Football." Over the next 14 years his broadcasts helped to increase the popularity of the National Football League.

Howard was often criticized for being too talkative and long-winded. He realized his failing and even made fun of his broadcasting style when he appeared in the Woody Allen movie *Bananas*.

In 1983, Howard was inducted into the Jewish Sports Hall of Fame in Israel. In that same year the Howard and Mary Edith [Howard's wife] Cosell Center for Physical Education was created in the couple's honor at Hebrew University, in Jerusalem.

Howard Cosell retired from sports broadcasting in early 1992.

ABC Radio Network

The Cigar and the Mouth, the two trademarks of sports broadcaster Howard Cosell.

Sidney Franklin
The First Jewish Bullfighter

Bullfighting is certainly an unlikely sport for a Jew to undertake. But Sidney Franklin did. Sidney was born in Brooklyn, New York, in 1903. His last name was actually Frumkin. He changed it to Franklin because he admired the famous American Benjamin Franklin. Sidney's parents were Russian Jewish immigrants. His father was a policeman. He was the fifth of their ten children.

Sidney was shy and the rumor spread that he had a weak heart. The neighborhood children intimidated him, so he stayed home a great deal. He took up bead embroidery as a hobby for which he won a prize at age 13.

When he was a child Sidney wanted to be an actor. At age 19, after an argument with his father, Sidney sailed to Mexico where he became interested in bullfighting, a popular sport in Mexico and Latin America, but not in the United States. Some Mexican friends told Sidney that no American could learn the sport. He took up the challenge and asked for instruction from the great Mexican bullfighter Rudolfo Gaona.

After several weeks of strenuous training, Sidney entered the ring for the first time on September 20, 1923, and became the first Jewish bullfighter. Though at first he seemed unsure of himself, he eventually killed the bull. "If you've got guts," he said, " you can do anything."

Horrified at Sidney for taking up bullfighting, his parents demanded that he give up his crazy antics and come home. He did not.

Instead, he went to Spain in 1929 and became the first American ever to engage in bullfighting there. He grew to be a popular sports figure in Spain, as well as in Portugal, Mexico, and parts of South America. Sometimes he earned as much as $100,000 a year, a vast sum at that time.

Sidney Franklin, the American Toreador of Brooklyn, after duel with bull in Seville, Spain.

Wide World Photos, Inc.

Sidney was naturally right-handed. But he taught himself to use the seven-pound sword with either hand when he was ready to kill the bull.

Getting ready for a bullfight was not easy. His matador's costume weighed 50 pounds and it took him an hour to dress for the fight.

His luck ran out in a bullfight in Madrid in 1930. The bull gored him so badly that he had to quit bullfighting for a number of years. He wrote his autobiography in 1952 and called it *The Bullfighter From Brooklyn.*

Why did Sidney Franklin like bullfighting so much? Because he loved the thrill of trying to outwit "an active opponent who can kill you if he catches you." He was referring, of course, to the bull!

Franklin died in New York in 1976.

Brad Gilbert

Top Jewish Tennis Player of the 1990s

Brad Gilbert was born in 1961 in Oakland, California. He came from a tennis-playing family; his sister Dana, who reached a world rank of 40, played on the pro tour for five years. Brad's older brother, Barry Jr., played tennis at the University of South Carolina.

Brad began playing tennis at age four, but as a teenager, Brad's small size proved a handicap. Bigger, stronger, and more talented players kept beating him. He agonized over defeat and reacted with temper tantrums. "He was a little tyrant," the late tennis star Arthur Ashe remembered. Brad nearly quit at 16 because he was so frustrated when he lost a match.

Gilbert studied at two California schools, first at Foothill Junior College, and then at Pepperdine University. He was an All-American tennis player and reached the finals of the 1982 National Collegiate Athletic Association (NCAA) championships. Following his junior year he turned pro.

Brad Gilbert captured his first pro title in Tapei in 1982 at the age of 21. By the end of 1982 he ranked 54 in the world. Two years later he leaped to No. 23 and in 1985 moved into the top 15 for the first time.

Brad has been successful because he possesses a good return of serve, accurate passing shots, and a strong forehand approach shot. He is highly disciplined and keeps diaries and charts on his matches that help him improve his game. His strategy is to force his opponent to play poorly. He calls it "winning ugly."

Brad Gilbert was ranked No. 21 at the end of 1986 when he earned $308,492. His best year was 1989 when he compiled a 17-match winning streak and won three consecutive tournaments. In August of that year he beat such

Israel Tennis Center

Another winner: Brad Gilbert, American tennis star of the 1990s.

top ten tennis pros as Michael Chang, Boris Becker, and Stefan Edberg and went on to win a Cincinnati, Ohio, tournament. He was ranked fifth in the world in 1989 and tenth in 1990.

Although in 1991 Brad failed to win a title for the first time since 1983, he did reach three finals and finished the year ranked 19th. It marked the sixth time in the last seven seasons that he finished in the top 20. His highest career rank was No. 4, on January 1, 1990.

Brad has been Boris Becker's biggest nemesis, beating the German tennis star four times. Off the court, Gilbert loves sports, especially basketball. "I'm a junkie for anything on the [sports] page."

Sidney Gillman
One of Football's Great Innovators

Sid Gillman, who coached pro football teams in the 1950s and 1960s, ranks as one of pro football's great innovators. He was the first coach to put the names of players on their jerseys. And he is one of the coaches who introduced the two-platoon system into modern football. Sid was the first coach to film practice sessions, sometimes watching them 18 hours a day. Once he was asked why he had done so well in pro football. He replied: "Because of the movie projector."

Born in 1911, he grew up in Minneapolis. He was co-captain of the 1932 Ohio State football team and was an All-American honorable mention in 1932 and 1933.

Among the football teams he coached in the 1930s and 1940s were Miami of Ohio and the University of Cincinnati. In 20 years of coaching in the Midwest, Gillman never won fewer than seven games a season.

Gillman became better known after coaching the National Football League (NFL) Los Angeles Rams between 1955 and 1959; then, the Los Angeles Chargers; and later the San Diego Chargers of the newly-formed American Football League (AFL). The very first year he coached the Rams, he led the team to a Western Division title.

In 1963, when his San Diego Chargers won the American Football League title, Gillman advocated a revolutionary idea: a "Super Bowl" game to be held between the AFL and the NFL title winner. At the time, the NFL rejected the idea, but the first Super Bowl was played four years later.

In 1967 Gillman's Chargers were considered to be the greatest offensive team in pro football history. They averaged an amazing 29 points per game, had an 11-3 record, and crushed the Boston Patriots in the AFL title game, 51-10.

Sid's teams won because he stressed use of the for-

Sid Gillman

Sid Gillman: one of the NFL's top coaches.

ward pass. His strategy succeeded because the opposing teams were very weak defensively.

In the 1970s Sid was executive vice president and general manager of the Houston Oilers. Appointing himself head coach, he led the vastly improved Oilers to a 7-7 record and was named Coach of the Year for 1974.

In 1982 Sid was assistant coach of the NFL's Philadelphia Eagles. The following year he was elected to the Pro Football Hall of Fame. Now retired, Sidney Gillman spends many hours watching football films and talking to young quarterbacks who seek his advice.

He is a member of the Jewish Sports Hall of Fame in Israel.

Hank Greenberg

Baseball Hero Who Refused to Play on Yom Kippur

Hank Greenberg, whose real name was Henry Benjamin Greenberg, was one of baseball's greatest right-handed sluggers. He was voted into the Baseball Hall of Fame in Cooperstown, New York, in 1956. He was the first Jew to be so honored.

Hank was born in New York City in 1911. He attended James Monroe High School in the Bronx where he was a star in four different sports. But he was best at baseball.

Hank's parents were Orthodox Jews and had little sympathy for their ball-playing son. They sometimes gazed outside their window at their son holding a baseball bat in his hand, and shouted in Yiddish, "Stickel Beltz," — "Lumber Bum."

As soon as Greenberg graduated from high school, baseball scouts tried to sign him for the major leagues. Hank's father, however, insisted he go to New York University. He attended briefly, the scouts still hounding him: Hank chose the Detroit Tigers over the New York Yankees, both of the American League, when a Tigers scout showed up for a Sabbath meal one Friday night at the Greenberg home and the Yankee scout failed to appear.

From 1933 to 1947, Greenberg played in the major leagues with the Tigers. He was then sold to the National League Pittsburgh Pirates where in 1947 he played out his last year in professional baseball.

Hank was one of baseball's greatest sluggers. During his major league career his batting average was .313. He had 1,628 hits of which 331 were home runs, eleven of them grandslammers. His career .605 slugging average ranks fifth on the all-time list.

The 1935 season was Hank's best season. He hit 36 homers, batted in 170 runs, and had 203 hits. He was voted the American League Most Valuable Player (MVP).

Greenberg, who was raised in an Orthodox family, proved his loyalty to Jewish tradition during the 1934 baseball season. The American League pennant race was very tight that year. A very important game was being played on Yom Kippur, but Hank refused to play, and instead went to the synagogue. The Detroit Tigers lost the game but won the pennant anyway. By showing his loyalty to his religion, Hank won the respect of the fans and the citizens of Detroit. The famous poet Edgar Guest praised Hank highly when he wrote a poem in which he said: "He's true to his religion, and I honor him for that."

TCMA

Hank Greenberg: one of baseball's greatest righthand sluggers.

The most exciting season of Hank Greenberg's career was 1938, when he came close to breaking Babe Ruth's 1927 record of sixty home runs in one season. With five games left to play, Greenberg had fifty-eight homers. He needed two more to tie and three more to break Ruth's record. But as hard as he tried, Hank couldn't hit another home run.

Hank Greenberg is a member of the Jewish Sports Hall of Fame in Israel. He died on September 4, 1986.

Marshall Holman
A Bowler for All Times

On the bowling alley, Marshall Holman wiggles, squirms, and leaps after nearly every throw. He talks, swears, and shouts at the pins. It is a system that seems to work.

Born in San Francisco in 1954, Marshall grew up in Medford, Oregon, where his father Philip was a disk jockey for radio station KFHA. After Phil did a show from the top of a flagpole in the early 1950s, he became known as "Holman the Poleman." His son Marshall believed that his tendency to be a "ham" came from his father. Needless to say, Marshall was nicknamed "Holman the bowlman."

Marshall began bowling at age 12, but only averaged 99 a game in his first year. Frequently, Marshall absented himself from high school much to his father's irritation. "I got a call from the high school principal every couple of weeks, wondering where Marshall was," Phil Holman said. "I knew exactly where he was. And I didn't really approve."

Despite his father, Marshall continued to bowl, though at first he was no star. Joining a pro bowling tour, he won only $500. For the next few years he bowled almost every day, playing at least 20 practice games.

Marshall Holman's first Professional Bowlers Association (PBA) tournament victory occurred in Fresno, California in 1973, during his second year on the tour. In 1979, he earned $107,255, and became the third player to win over $100,000 in one year.

Marshall has a temper. He was put on probation for six months after a 1979 Seattle tournament during which he kicked a chair and a ball rack and then threw pencils when the match went against him. The following year, he was barred from ten tournaments as punishment for kicking a light on a lane after failing to obtain a much needed

He won more than 20 pro titles: Marshall Holman aiming for another triumph.

Professional Bowlers Association

tenth frame strike.

He had an excellent year in 1981, earning $122,880. In 1986 he won his second Firestone Tournament of Champions and earned the largest check in PBA history, $50,000. That took him over the $1 million mark in total career earnings, only the third player in PBA history to do so. Mark Roth and Earl Anthony were the other two.

Though he did not win a tournament in 1987, Holman won the coveted PBA Player of the Year award. He was also awarded the George Young High Average Award for the third time, leading the Tour with a 216.8 per game average. He earned that award in 1982 and 1984 as well. In 1988, Holman won his 21st PBA title.

Marshall Holman has earned $1.4 million in the course of his career. He is only one of six bowlers to win over 20 bowling championships. As a result, Marshall was inducted into the Professional Bowling Association's Hall of Fame in 1990.

Nat Holman

Inventor of the Basketball Pivot Play

Nat Holman, who is only 5 feet, 11 inches tall, is considered one of the greatest basketball players of all time. Holman was born in 1896 in New York City. He came from an athletic family: four brothers played basketball, two, soccer. It was in the parks and playgrounds on the lower East Side of New York City that Nat Holman learned to play baseball and basketball. He was a good enough baseball player to receive an offer to play with the National League's Cincinnati Reds, but he turned them down to concentrate on basketball.

Nat played with a professional basketball team called the Original Celtics from 1921 to 1929. He was called the finest ball handler, playmaker, and set-shot artist of his day. With Nat on their team, the Original Celtics rarely lost a game. For instance, they were 193-11 in 1922 and 204-11 in 1923. The team joined the American Basketball League, but broke up in 1929 because there was no serious competition for them.

Nat Holman is famous for inventing the pivot play, one of the most important plays in basketball. It caused a revolution in the game. Holman would feint the person who was guarding him out of position and run him into the pivot or post. Nat would then cut by the guard where Nat would receive a short give-and-go pass, and lay up an easy basket.

Besides playing the game, Nat coached basketball. From 1920 to 1953 he was the coach of the City College of New York (CCNY) basketball team. He also coached CCNY in 1955, 1957 and 1959. Nat's coaching record for his entire career was 422 wins and only 188 losses.

Nat's most successful season as a basketball coach came in 1949-50 when his CCNY Beavers won both major

Holman at blackboard going over plays with CCNY squad (November 3, 1954).

Jewish Sports Hall of Fame.

tournaments in college basketball: the National Invitation Tournament (NIT) and the NCAA playoffs. No other coach had accomplished that feat.

Holman has always been proud of being Jewish. "Some of what I heard and learned sitting next to my father in the synagogue rubbed off on me," he once said. Nat was the first American coach to go to Israel. He went there in 1949, a year after the State was founded, to teach Israelis how to play basketball.

In 1967 Nat was elected to the Basketball Hall of Fame. In 1978 the Wingate Institute in Israel dedicated the Nat Holman School for Coaches and Instructors. He was inducted into the Jewish Sports Hall of Fame in Israel in 1981.

Irving Jaffee
Champion Speed Skater

Irving Jaffee, who became famous as a champion speed skater, actually wanted to be a baseball star as a youngster. But when he failed to make the baseball team at DeWitt Clinton High School in New York City, Irving became so angry that he left school.

Irving's parents came from Russia to New York in 1898. Irving's father found work operating a pushcart. Eight years later Irving was born.

After dropping out of high school, Irving tried boxing. In his very first fight he was knocked out. He quit the ring. Irving tried ice skating for the first time when some friends took him to the Ice Palace rink in New York City. He had a hard time keeping his balance. His sister gave him his first pair of ice skates, but they were three sizes too large and he had to wear nine pairs of socks to make them fit. He began to love skating, especially speed skating, and always carried a pair of skates under his arm.

At first he was shy about entering skating competitions. He felt that ice skating was not for Jews. His friends convinced him that, with his speed, he should compete. He agreed, but lost nine of the first ten races he entered. It was only after the great skater Norval Bapte advised him that his skates were too large that Irving improved.

Eventually he won the five-mile national championship at Saranac Lake in 1927 and broke the world record. Winning that race made him eligible for the 1928 Winter Olympics—or so it seemed. The United States Olympic Committee did not want to send Jaffee to the St. Moritz, Switzerland, Winter Olympics. Committee members believed he would be no match for the Scandinavian skaters. But in the end, the Committee decided to let Jaffee join the team. The ship had to be delayed so that Jaffee could get his visa and a passport.

Jewish Sports Hall of Fame, Netanya, Israel

February 1932, Lake Placid, New York. Four Olympic gold medalists gather at a dinner in their honor at the 1932 Lake Placid, Winter Olympic Games. From left: Jaffee, Karl Schaeffer, Germany (men's figure skating gold medal winner), Sonja Henie, Norway (women's figure skating gold medal winner), and Jack Shea of Lake Placid (500- and 1500-meter gold medal winner for speed skating).

Jaffee did not win a gold medal at St. Moritz, but many thought he deserved to win the 10,000-meter race, which was called off in the middle when the ice began to melt. Jaffee had the fastest time among those in the race.

Because he had to care for his sick mother, Jaffee did not train much for the 1932 Winter Olympics, which were held at Lake Placid, New York. Still, he won both the 5,000- and the 10,000-meter skating races. He died in San Diego, California, in 1981, the same year that he was inducted into the Jewish Sports Hall of Fame in Israel.

Irena Kirszenstein-Szewinska

Greatest Woman Track and Field Star

Irena was born in 1946 in Leningrad to Polish parents who had fled to Russia during World War II. She and her parents eventually settled in Warsaw.

After Irena's athletic ability had been recognized at school, her mother encouraged her to join a local sports club where she developed into a sprinter and long jumper.

At age 18, Irena surprised everyone at the 1964 Tokyo Olympics by winning three medals: a gold one as a member of Poland's 400-meter relay team, which set a world record of 43.6 seconds; a silver one for her long jump of 21 feet, 7 1/2 inches; and a silver one in the 200-meter dash, with a near record of 23.1 seconds.

While pursuing her athletic career, Irena studied economics at Warsaw University.

In 1965 Irena was named Poland's Athlete of the Year. Tass, the official Russian news agency, also voted her the outstanding woman athlete in the world.

Millions of Poles admired her and followed her career. Often, she was stopped on Warsaw streets to sign autographs. Because she was so popular, some anti-Semitic Poles found it convenient to forget that Irena was Jewish.

In 1968, at the Olympics in Mexico City, Irena won a gold medal in the 200-meter Olympic race, setting a new world record of 22.5 seconds. She also won a bronze medal in the 100-meter race.

Irena put her career on hold when her son, Andrzej, was born in February 1970, but in 1974 made a strong comeback, chopping a tenth of a second off her 200-meter world mark, running it in 22.4 seconds. She also recorded the second fastest time for a woman in the 100-meters: a

10.9 second sprint.

In that year (1974), she was voted United Press International Sportswoman of the Year. *Track and Field News* named her Woman Athlete of the Year.

At the 1976 Montreal Olympics, Irena won her seventh Olympic medal by capturing the 400-meter race, setting a new world record of 49.29, and improving upon her own world record by almost half a second.

When asked if her Olympic victories were a triumph for the Communist system, she replied: "I know the people of Poland were very happy to see the Polish flag flying highest. But I run because it gives me great pleasure and satisfaction. I run for me."

Her total of seven Olympic (three of them gold) and 10 European (five gold) medals is a record that has no rival in the history of women's track and field.

Irena Kirszenstein-Szewinska is a member of the Jewish Sports Hall of Fame in Israel.

Jewish Sports Hall of Fame

Irena Kirszenstein-Szewinska—track and field star.

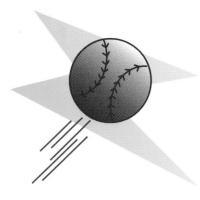

Sandy Koufax

One of Baseball's Greatest Pitchers

Sandy Koufax was one of the greatest baseball pitchers of all time. He was awarded the top honor given a major league pitcher (the Cy Young Award) three times in four seasons. In 1972 he was the youngest player ever admitted to the Baseball Hall of Fame.

Born in 1935 in the Borough Park section of Brooklyn, to Jack and Evelyn Braun, Sandy's given name was Sanford. At age three, his parents divorced. Sandy and his mother lived with her parents for some time. When Sandy was nine, his mother remarried. Sandy took the name Koufax, the name of his stepfather, whom he loved very much and thought of as his real father.

Sandy was an outstanding basketball player at Lafayette High School but he turned to baseball during his senior year because so many of his friends were on the team. He played first base.

On July 6, 1955, Sandy began his professional career playing for the Brooklyn Dodgers. In this, his first season, he shut out the Cincinnati Reds on two hits and struck out 14 batters. This was the most strikeouts in one game by any National League pitcher that year.

Despite these feats, during the first six seasons southpaw Koufax was pitching for the Dodgers he won only 36 games (and lost 40). He did have one day of glory in 1959. It was the day on which he struck out 18 batters, tying the major league record set two decades earlier by Cleveland Indian pitcher Bob Feller.

In 1960, when Sandy had a pitching record of only eight wins and 13 losses, he almost quit. But in 1961 he roared back, winning 18 games and losing only 13. He also struck out 269 batters, breaking a National League record held by the legendary Christy Mathewson.

Over the next six seasons, Koufax won 129 games and lost only 47. He had a pitching record of 25-5 in 1963 and 19-5 in 1964; 26-7 in 1965; and 27-9 in 1966. On September 9, 1965, Koufax pitched a perfect game against the Chicago Cubs. This was one of only 14 perfect games pitched in baseball history.

Sandy's Jewishness was tested on opening day of the World Series in October 1965 when the Dodgers played the Minnesota Twins. It was Yom Kippur, the holiest day of the Jewish year. Sandy did not come to the ballpark. The Dodgers lost 8-2. A sports columnist criticized Sandy for not pitching that day. But Sandy pitched the seventh and deciding game, and the Dodgers won the World Series. To Sandy, winning the World Series was sweet revenge for the columnist's unkind words.

After the 1966 season, Koufax's career was cut short due to a sore arm. In the course of his career he had struck out 2,396 batters and pitched 40 shutouts. He also set a major league record for the most seasons (three) with 300 or more strikeouts. He was the first pitcher in the major leagues to pitch four no-hit games. Only Nolan Ryan—with seven—has more no-hitters.

Sandy Koufax is a member of the Jewish Sports Hall of Fame in Israel.

Zvi Nishri, Physical Education and Sports Archives of the Wingate Institute of Physical Education and Sport, Netanya, Israel

Wind-up to pitch: Sandy Koufax, the marvelous pitcher of the 1960s.

Aaron Krickstein
Marathon Man of Tennis

Aaron Krickstein rose to the heights of professional tennis faster than anyone else. Aaron was born in Ann Arbor, Michigan in 1967. His father Herbert is a pathologist at Detroit's St. John's Hospital. His grandfather was a rabbi.

At the ages of five and six, he won the Michigan state swimming titles in the freestyle and butterfly. Had he pursued a swimming career, Aaron could have been one of America's top swimmers.

But Aaron preferred the courts to the pool and at age six began playing tennis. As a junior player he never lost to anyone younger than himself.

In 1982 Aaron began training under the famous tennis coach Nick Bollettieri in Bradenton, Florida. During the next three years, Bollettieri helped Aaron to develop his hard-hitting style, particularly his powerful forehand and strong baseline game.

Aaron began playing on the circuit in early 1983. At the U.S. Open that fall, he managed the incredible feat of reaching the Final 16. In the opening round he defeated Stefan Edberg in five sets in a tie-break.

Turning pro soon afterward, Krickstein was aware of his youth. "I was kind of afraid to talk to the guys. I felt so young. In the locker rooms, I felt out of place. But then I started winning some matches....I learned a lot."

Aaron won his first professional title in October 1983, capturing the Tel Aviv Grand Prix at the age of 16. That made him the youngest player ever to win a professional tennis title.

Impressed with Aaron, a reporter asked Herb Krickstein if he thought his son might play for the Israeli Davis Cup team. Aaron's dad paused, then noted that what he and Aaron had in mind was that someday his son might play for the American Davis Cup team.

Young Krickstein was ranked eighth in the world in 1989, 20th in 1990, and 34th in 1991. His official career earnings came to $2,081,838.

German tennis star Boris Becker once said of Aaron Krickstein: "He is a tough player. He never really gives up, and that's his best point." Indeed, Aaron is known on the tour as "Marathon Man" because he does so well in five-set matches.

In 1989 Krickstein finished eighth and played most of 1990 with several nagging injuries, ending the year ranked at 20. His best career rank was No. 6 on February 26, 1990. He ended 1991 at 34 and during 1992 was in the 20s and 30s.

He has won seven singles titles during his professional career.

Israel Tennis Center

Aaron Krickstein (right) with Brad Gilbert after a recent Tel Aviv Grand Prix tournament at the Israel Tennis Center, Ramat Hasharon, Israel.

Benny Leonard

Best Jewish Boxer in History

Benny Leonard was the most famous Jewish personality in America of his era. He became a legend partly because of his claim that no one had ever messed his slicked-down hair in over 200 boxing matches.

Leonard's real name was Benjamin Leiner. He was born in 1896 in New York City. As a youngster growing up in a Jewish neighborhood, he frequently got into fistfights with the children of Italian and Irish immigrants. He fought not only with fists but also with sticks, stones, and bottles. Once he beat up a group of non-Jews who had attacked an elderly Jewish woman. Another time he took on hoodlums who had tried to deface a synagogue. In part because of some of the beatings he took, that kind of fighting did not appeal to him.

But he did find that he liked fighting with gloves, which he tried for the first time at age 11. At first his parents did not understand why he wanted to box. Benny's mother asked him, weeping, "A prizefighter you want to be? Is that a life for a respectable man? For a Jew?"

For Benny it certainly was. He used the name "Benny Leonard" in his early fights so his parents would not know that he was boxing. They found out, however. Benny made sure to call them after every fight. Once, however, his father hung up immediately upon learning that his son was calling all the way from Cleveland to New York!

Benny's warmest feelings were reserved for his mom. He always carried her photo with him, and to make her happy, he never fought on a Jewish holiday.

Benny Leonard's first boxing victory occurred in 1915 when he defeated veteran Joe Mandot. Two years later he knocked out Freddy Welsh and became lightweight champion.

He held the world lightweight title from 1917 to 1924.

His career record was 88 wins (68 by knockout) and only five losses. On January 15, 1925, Leonard retired. "My mother was so happy," he recalled. "I was 29, practically a millionaire, and without a scratch."

He bought a hockey team, played in vaudeville, and taught boxing at City College in New York. After the 1929 stock market crash wiped out all his savings, Leonard tried a comeback as a welterweight boxer. He was eager to defeat a hard-hitting Irish fighter named Jimmy McLarnin, who had a reputation for conquering Jewish boxers in the ring. But, when they fought on October 7, 1932, McLarnin had little trouble defeating Leonard, then 35 years old.

In 1947, working as a referee at New York's St. Nicholas Arena one evening, he collapsed and died of a brain hemorrhage. The greatest tribute to Benny came from a newspaper editor Arthur Brisbane who said: "He has done more to conquer anti-Semitism than a thousand textbooks."

Benny Leonard is a member of the Jewish Sports Hall of Fame in Israel.

Zvi Nishri, Physical Education and Sport Archives of the Wingate Institute of Physical Education and Sport, Netanya, Israel

Squaring off: Benny Leonard shows how he became a boxing legend.

Marv Levy
Head Coach of the Buffalo Bills

Marv Levy has been a highly-successful profession-al football coach since the 1970s. As head coach of the NFL Buffalo Bills since 1986, Marv has taken his team to the Super Bowl three times between the 1990 and 1992 seasons. Unfortunately for Levy, the Bills lost all three times: in 1990 to the New York Giants, 20-19, in 1991 to the Washington Redskins, 37-24, and in 1992 to the Dallas Cowboys, 52-17.

Marv, who was born in Chicago, Illinois in 1928, dropped out of Harvard Law School in 1951 to take a junior varsity coaching job at Country Day School in St. Louis. When he telephoned his father with the news, there was silence on the other end of the line. Then Marv's dad said, "You better be a good coach."

Marv became head coach of the Montreal Alouettes in the Canadian Football League in 1973. The Alouettes won the Canadian Football League Grey Cup twice (1974 and 1977) during Levy's five years as coach. His coaching record for those five years was 50-34-4.

He became head coach of the NFL's Kansas City Chiefs in 1978, compiling a 31-42 won-lost record over the next four years. His strategy was to rebuild Kansas City's defense. "Offense sells tickets," he told a news conference, "defense wins games." After three mediocre seasons (4-12; 7-9; 8-8) and a good one (9-7) in 1981, the Chiefs let Levy go.

Taking over the Buffalo Bills in midseason of 1986, Levy had a record of only 2-5. The turnaround came in 1988 when the Bills were 12-4. Levy has led the Bills to four American Football Conference East titles as well as two AFC championships. His overall coaching record with the Bills has been 75-38.

Obsessive about planning for a game, Coach Levy sometimes stays up to 4 a.m. to map out game plans. He encourages his teams to run the ball and dislikes fancy offensive schemes.

Levy has been known to occasionally use complicated words such as "clandestine," "debacle," and "slovenly" in his pep talks. Some Buffalo players write the tongue-twisters in their play notebooks so they can look up the words later.

Marv insists he is no intellectual. "I'm a coach. I always felt good around other coaches. I'm one of them. I'm not a professor."

Buffalo Bills

The Wise Old Man of Pro Football: Marv Levy, head coach of the NFL's Buffalo Bills.

Sid Luckman

Great Quarterback and Football Brain

Sid Luckman's father gave him a football in 1924 when the boy was eight years old.

At Columbia University Sid became one of the outstanding triple-threat men in college football. He could run, pass and punt. Even though the Columbia team did not have a winning season, Sid made All-American in his senior year in 1938.

Although Luckman intended to enter the family trucking business after graduating from college, he was drafted by the NFL's Chicago Bears. After Bears owner George Halas pleaded with Sid to join his team, Sid agreed.

Though in college Luckman had always played tailback, he switched to quarterback in the new T-formation pioneered by the Bears. Wherever he was, he spent hours practicing pivots, feints, handoffs, and ball handling: in the dressing room, at home, in hotels on road trips, and even on vacation between seasons. In the 1940s, he ranked as the greatest long-range passer of his era.

Luckman's best year was 1943. On November 14, playing at the Polo Grounds in New York, he passed for a record seven touchdowns against the New York Giants. "Strictly luck," Luckman said modestly. The 28 touchdowns Sid tossed in 10 games in 1943 remained a record until the Baltimore Colts' Johnny Unitas broke it in 1959 with 32 in 12 games.

Luckman was a genius at football strategy and led the Chicago Bears, for whom he played from 1939 to 1947, to five Western Conference titles and four National Football League championships (in 1940, 1941, 1943, and 1946).

During World War II, when Sid Luckman served in the U.S. Navy, he was assigned to an oil tanker cruising the

Atlantic. At times he got shore leave to play for the Bears. Despite the Bears' weak season in 1945, Luckman shared the passing title with player Sammy Baugh and led the league in touchdown passes (14) and yardage gained (1,725).

In 1949, two years after he retired, Sid was asked by a reporter whether he was religious. "Well, yes," was his answer. "I go to the temple regularly and I observe the High Holidays and I never go to bed at night without saying a little prayer."

Luckman was selected to join the Pro Football Hall of Fame in 1965. He is also a member of the Jewish Sports Hall of Fame in Israel. Lou Little, his former coach at Columbia, said of Sid: "He was a great passer, of course, and a great football brain, but people forget he was a great leader."

Zvi Nishri, Physical Education and Sport Archives of the Wingate Institute of Physical Education and Sport, Netanya, Israel

Tossing touchdowns and breaking records: Sid Luckman, former NFL hero.

Amos Mansdorf
Israel's Best Tennis Player

When he was six years old, Amos Mansdorf watched his parents play tennis on the only court at the Herzylia Country Club. He wanted to play too. Club officials told him that he had to wait until he was ten. Amos couldn't wait that long.

Born in Tel Aviv in 1965, when he was nine years old, Amos read a newspaper announcement that the Tel Aviv University Tennis Club was searching for young talent. He applied, but was rejected. That rejection made him hesitate even two years later to try out for the children's program at the newly built Israel Tennis Center in Ramat Hasharon near Tel Aviv. His mother, however, convinced him to go. She acted wisely.

A few months later, it was time for the family vacation to Greece. "I think I'll skip it," Amos told his parents. "I would rather stay here with Grandma and play tennis." When his parents returned from their holiday, Amos announced at the dinner table, "I'm worried. When I play at Wimbledon, how will I adjust to grass?"

In 1983, as a senior in high school, he won the Asian Junior Championship in Hong Kong, reaching a world adult ranking of 250. In early 1984, he began his three-year stint in the Israeli army and was frustrated by the fact that he was doing guard duty while non-Israeli tennis players were practicing tennis. When possible, he sandwiched in practice and play in international tournaments. In November 1985 he won the South African Open, his first Grand Prix tournament triumph. Amazingly, when he left the army in February 1987 Amos held a rank of 36.

Though hardly a John McEnroe, Amos Mansdorf has a temper on the tennis court. He has broken rackets, whined about line calls, and stomped off the court. He

was dismissed from the Israeli Davis Cup team in
May 1992 for refusing to
follow orders during training.

Amos had a great
year in 1987. In a Davis
Cup match in March, he
won two singles victories,
helping Israel upset Czech-
oslovakia. Amos called
those triumphs his "best
moment" in tennis. *World
Tennis* magazine named
him the most improved
player on the men's tour
that same year.

Mansdorf is the best
tennis player Israel has
ever produced. In Novem-
ber 16, 1987, he reached his
highest career rank: 18th
in the world. In 1988 he
ranked 26th; 39th in 1989;
and 33rd in 1990.

Returning to Israel af-
ter the Persian Gulf war

Israel Tennis Center

**Israel's top
tennis success:
Amos Mansdorf
on center court
in Israel.**

began in January 1991, Amos temporarily suspended his
tennis activity. "How will it look to the public if I go on
playing and they're sitting in their gas masks?" That year
his ranking dropped to 62, but by early 1992, after winning 12 matches in three tournaments, he climbed back
to near the top 20 in the world.

Daniel Mendoza

Father of Modern Boxing and Star of Israel

Daniel Mendoza, the most famous Jewish sportsman of the late 18th and early 19th century, was the father of modern boxing. Before Mendoza, boxing had consisted of little more than brutal punching. But he introduced new punches and strategies and emphasized the need for footwork and sparring. He also devised defensive moves that enabled him to fight against much heavier opponents.

Daniel was born in 1764 in London, England and spent much of his young life defending Judaism—often with his bare fists. After his bar mitzvah, Daniel wanted to become a glazier, but he whipped the glazier's son in a fight and lost his job. Daniel's father tried in vain to curb his son's fondness for brawls. He quickly developed a reputation as a fearless street fighter.

Although he was only 5 feet, 7 inches tall, and weighed 160 pounds, he had an enormous chest and was never afraid to fight larger men.

Mendoza's chief boxing rival was a man named Richard Humphreys. Mendoza promised himself he would quit the ring after he defeated Humphreys.

Mendoza lost his first fight to Humphreys on January 9, 1788. To avoid bodily punishment, Mendoza worked out a new style, using sidestepping, a straight left, and special guarding techniques. Some complained, however, that Mendoza had adopted the cowardly manner of running away from his rival.

Finally on May 6, 1789, Mendoza defeated Humphreys. And England had a new hero! Songs were written about him. And the next year, after the two men fought again, and Mendoza won easily, Daniel became known as "The Star of Israel."

When he fought his first professional fight in 1790, he

was victorious. The victory won him the patronage of the Prince of Wales. Being accepted by royalty helped elevate the position of the Jew in English society. Mendoza was proud of his heritage and billed himself as "Mendoza the Jew."

After having defeated the best fighters around, Daniel was recognized as world heavyweight champion and reigned as such from 1791 to 1795. In the early 1790s, boxing was so popular that Mendoza was persuaded to open a small theater in London where he gave public sparring exhibitions and taught others how to box.

Zvi Nishri, Physical Education and Sport Archives of the Wingate Institute of Physical Education and Sport, Netanya, Israel

Daniel Mendoza (left) fighting his archrival Richard Humphreys.

By 1820, at age 56, Mendoza was no longer a great fighter. Still he continued to box. After watching him lose to a much younger man, an anonymous poet wrote sadly: "Is this Mendoza? Is this the Jew of whom my fancy cherished so beautiful a waking dream?"

In 1789 Mendoza wrote *The Art of Boxing,* and in 1816 *The Memoirs of the Life of Daniel Mendoza.* Mendoza had become a wealthy man, but he gave away so much money that he died poor, leaving a wife and 11 children. In 1965 he was in the first group of fighters chosen to be honored in the Boxing Hall of Fame in the United States. He is also a member of the Jewish Sports Hall of Fame in Israel.

Al "Flip" Rosen

Outstanding Baseball Player and Astute General Manager

Al Rosen was born in 1925 in Spartanburg, South Carolina. When Al was a child, his mother and father were divorced. Al and his brother Jerry were raised by their mother, who worked as a saleswoman in a dress shop.

From the age of one, Al suffered from violent asthma attacks. On doctor's orders, Al was urged to play outside as much as possible. This led to his love affair with sports. But his mother was terribly upset as she watched him breathe heavily, as if each breath would be his last.

Eventually, the asthma was cured, and Al went on to become one of the best third basemen in baseball history. Al became the only Jewish boy in his neighborhood when his family moved to Miami, Florida. Non-Jewish youngsters hurled anti-Semitic slurs at Al, angering him. "I took my share of whippings, but I learned how to take care of myself."

Al also played football, basketball, and won the middleweight boxing title in a Florida high school tournament. Baseball, however, was his first love. He was an All-City third baseman at Miami High School.

He obtained his lifetime nickname of "Flip" as a softball pitcher, because of the way he "flipped" the ball to the batter. He played in the minor leagues between 1946 and 1949. In 1947 he hit .347, playing with an Oklahoma team in the Texas League. Weak fielding skills slowed his march to the majors.

He finally made the majors in 1950, when the Cleveland Indians signed him. That year he hit .287, slugged 37 homers, and knocked in 116 runs. He won Rookie of the Year honors.

Al Rosen was the first unanimous selection for Most Valuable Player when he won the award in 1953.

Ed Sullivan, the *New York Daily News* columnist and television star, wrote that Rosen was of Jewish parentage, but a practicing Catholic. "At the plate," said Sullivan, "you'll notice he makes the sign of the cross with his bat." Rosen denied the story, insisting that he was a proud Jew.

Rosen refused to play baseball on the High Holy Days. In 1953 he might have won the batting title had he played on those Jewish holidays and gotten a few hits. Nevertheless, despite missing a few games that year, he did win the Home Run Crown with 43 homers, and the RBI title with 145. He knocked in over 100 runs in each season between 1950 and 1954.

San Francisco Giants

Going for the bleachers: Al Rosen, third-base star of the 1950s, belts another home run.

Plagued by injuries, Al retired in 1956 and since then has worked in the front office of several major league clubs, including the Indians, the Yankees, and Houston Astros. Since 1985 he has been president and general manager of the San Francisco Giants. In 1987, after the Giants won their first National League West championship in 16 years, Rosen was voted Major League Executive of the Year by *The Sporting News.*

Al Rosen is a member of the Jewish Sports Hall of Fame in Israel.

Barney Ross

Jewish Champion Boxer Who Was Never Knocked Out

Barney Ross had much to overcome as a boxer. One large obstacle was his mother who did not want him to fight. To avoid offending her, Barney concealed his boxing career by changing his name from Barnet David Rosofsky to Barney Ross. But when she realized how good he was inside the ring, she supported his career.

His entire life was a struggle—inside and outside the boxing ring.

Barney was born in 1909 on the lower East Side of New York City, the son of Russian immigrants who had come to the United States six years earlier. When he was two, his parents moved to the Jewish section of Chicago. His father Isadore, a Talmudic scholar, made sure the Rosofsky's two-and-a-half room home had an Orthodox atmosphere. When Barney was only 14, his father was killed by two holdup men who broke into the family grocery store.

Unable to provide for her children, Barney's mother suffered a nervous breakdown. His two younger brothers and sister were placed in an orphanage. Barney and an older brother went to live with a cousin.

As a youngster, Barney wanted to become a Hebrew teacher. But after his father's death he felt responsible to care for his mother, his three brothers, and a sister. He wanted to make money quickly. "Everything that happened to me afterward," he wrote, "happened because of that senseless, stupid murder." He even became a minor racketeer and at one point acted as a messenger for the notorious Al Capone gang.

But in 1926, just before he turned 18, Barney's interests turned to boxing. Soon thereafter, he captured the featherweight title in the New York-Chicago Golden Gloves tournament, and he decided to turn professional.

Seven years later he defeated the lightweight champion Tony Canzoneri. The new champion missed the post-fight celebration: he had to walk his mother, by now an enthusiastic supporter of her son's career, home from the stadium. It was Friday night, the Jewish Sabbath, and Mrs. Rosofsky, a religious woman, would not ride.

Ross defended his lightweight title five times. But, as he grew older and heavier, he began to eye the welterweight division. On May 30, 1934, after a fifteen-round battle with the reigning champion, Jimmy "Baby Face" McLarnin, Barney won a split decision and the welterweight title.

Barney Ross was the first boxer to hold the lightweight and welterweight crowns at the same time. From 1933 to 1935 Barney was the world lightweight and junior welterweight champion. He was also world welterweight champion from 1934 to 1938.

His career ended in 1938 after he fought 329 times without ever being knocked out. As a marine during World War II, Ross caught malaria. He used morphine to ease the pain and soon became addicted to it. He overcame his addiction and in 1946 was pronounced cured.

Ross died in 1967. He is a member of the Jewish Sports Hall of Fame in Israel.

Ring Magazine

Barney Ross: the first boxer to hold the lightweight and welterweight crowns at the same time.

Esther Shachamorov Roth
Israel's Outstanding Track Star

When Esther Roth was 18 years old, she was one of the best women track stars in the hurdles. She held the world record (7.1 seconds) for the 60-meter indoor hurdles for one day.

Esther was born in Tel Aviv in 1952. Her parents emigrated from Moscow to Palestine in 1940. Before she married Peter Roth in 1973, she was known by her birth name, Esther Shachamorov.

At the 1970 Asian Games in Bangkok, she won gold medals in the hurdles and pentathlon events and a silver medal in the long jump. She broke Israeli records in numerous track and field events, including the 100- and 200-meter races, long jump, and pentathlon. In 1972 she was a member of the Israeli contingent at the Munich Olympics.

Esther had reached the 100-meter semifinals when Palestinian Arab terrorists attacked the Munich Olympic village, killing 11 Israeli team members. Esther and the rest of the women's team escaped harm because their quarters were in a separate building 200 meters from their male teammates. Because Esther's coach, Amitzur Shapira, was one of those killed, Esther considered hanging up her track shoes permanently.

She returned to competition in 1973, winning the 100-meter, 200-meter, and long jump at the Maccabiah Games. At the time she was three months pregnant but didn't know it. Nor did the doctors. Though her son Yaron was born in February 1974, Esther dominated the 1974 Asian Games seven months later, winning three gold medals in the 200-meter dash, the 100-meter hurdles, and the 100-meter sprint.

At the 1976 Olympics in Montreal, Esther reached the finals of the 100-meter hurdles, coming in sixth. The first Israeli to reach an Olympic finals, she set a new Israeli rec-

Esther Roth (center) leaps to another track victory in the finals of the 100-meter hurdles at the 9th Hapoel games.

Israel Government Press Office

ord of 13.04 seconds for the event. The 1976 Olympics showed that she was the greatest woman hurdler outside of Eastern Europe. Montreal was her last major international competition. She was named Sportsman of the Year in Israel three times by the Israeli newspaper *Ma'ariv*.

Esther retired in September 1979, but a month later she was persuaded to compete in the Moscow Olympics the following summer. However, she did not participate in those games because Israel joined the United States boycott of that Olympic meet.

Esther now teaches physical education at a junior high school in Ra'anana, near Tel Aviv. Besides their son, Yaron, Esther and Peter have an eight-year-old daughter Michal.

Mark Roth

Bowling Superstar

Mark Roth was born in Brooklyn, New York, in 1951. Mark began to bowl because he was too small for football or basketball. He often spent Saturday nights alone, practicing at the bowling alley until two a.m. His mother tried to convince him that bowling was worthless, but she did not succeed. He told her the bowling lanes were better for him than the street corner. Her opinion changed when he began earning money from the sport.

When Mark began to bowl at age 11 he did not take enough time before releasing the ball. He simply stood up and threw the ball. He took a few extra steps in order to give the ball more speed.

After four years on the pro bowling tour, he won his first event: the King Louis, in Kansas City, in 1975. Two years later he was the best bowler on the pro tour with an average of 218.174.

Mark throws the ball unusually fast, with a power rarely seen at a bowling alley. At one time, his tight grip used to tear the skin off his right thumb, but he has since learned to protect his hand.

Mark Roth urges young pros to take four or five smooth steps, to refrain from hooking the ball too much, and to keep arms straight and close to the body. To prepare for a day at the lanes, Mark goes through a routine in his hotel room that consists of shrieks and punching the air, all to release emotional tension.

He won four PBA events in 1983 and had earnings that year of $158,712. In 1984 he won four American Bowling Association (ABA) Championship titles. In 1986 he said, "I'll never win the ABA's Sportsmanship Award. You have to be too nice. Bowlers who are nice don't have enough killer instinct. I'd rather win than be nice."

In the late 1980s Roth was less successful; he earned

Going for the strike: Mark Roth eyes another championship.

Professional Bowlers Association

$81,375 in 1988, but only $11,190 in 1991. He has been plagued with injuries, including tendinitis in his right wrist and a foot ailment that required corrective surgery.

Mark has won 34 Professional Bowlers Association titles. He has been named PBA Player of the Year four times: in 1977, 1978, 1979, and 1984. His 215-plus average between 1976 and 1990 was the best long-term average in PBA history.

In 1992 Mark Roth was elected to the Jewish Sports Hall of Fame in Israel.

Angelica Rozeanu
Greatest Woman Table Tennis Player

Angelica was born in Bucharest in 1921. When she was nine years old, Angelica and her brother Gaston, then 16, put up a net on the dining room table and he taught her how to play table tennis. His lessons paid off.

She later won 17 world titles, and is considered the greatest woman table tennis player in history. She won six of those titles consecutively, from 1950 to 1955.

In 1936, Angelica met the great Hungarian table tennis star Victor Barna, and decided to adopt his backhand drive.

When she was 15, Angelica won her first important event, the Rumanian National Women's Championship in Chernovitz, Rumania. She captured that title every year thereafter until 1957, except for the war years—1940-1945—when she did not compete. The Nazis, in control of Rumania during the war, banned Jews from entering sports centers, effectively preventing Angelica from playing table tennis.

In 1944, Angelica married fellow Rumanian Lou Rozeanu. In 1948 she failed to win the World Championships in Wembley (in London, England) and Angelica decided to change her tactics from defensive to offensive play. She began to practice a surprise attack from both sides. Her strong forehand drive was now complemented by an excellent backhand.

In Budapest, Hungary, in 1950, she won the first of her six straight world singles titles. Two years later she became Rumania's national table tennis coach and held that post until 1958.

In 1956, Rozeanu competed in the Women's World Championships in Tokyo. There she hoped to win an unprecedented seventh straight world title. In a tense, close

Zvi Nishri, Physical Education and Sport Archives of the Wingate Institute
of Physical Education and Sport, Netanya, Israel

Angelica Rozeanu, Romanian table tennis phenomenon (right) during a practice session.

match described as the best in the history of table tennis, she lost to an unknown Japanese player, Kiyoko Tasaka, 21-19, 22-20, and 32-30. Angelica called the defeat the worst disappointment of her career.

During 1959 and 1960, when the post of chairman of the National Table Tennis Federation in Rumania was held by a Nazi-oriented Communist, a purge of Jewish table tennis players began. Angelica was banned from playing in international matches. She and her daughter Michaela, then 14, immigrated to Israel in 1960, joining her husband who had moved there earlier.

In 1961, Angelica won the Maccabiah Games table tennis championships. She continued to win singles and doubles titles in Europe, but by 1962 Israeli sports authorities, pleading a lack of funds, refused to send her abroad anymore. Angry and disappointed, she gave up the game, having won some 100 international titles during her career.

Angelica Rozeanu is a member of the Jewish Sports Hall of Fame in Israel.

Richard "Dick" Savitt

Only Jew to Win a Wimbledon Singles

Dick was born in 1927 in Bayonne, New Jersey. As a youngster he was interested in football, baseball, basketball—but not tennis. He took up tennis at age 13 after ball-boying at the Berkeley Tennis Club in Orange, New Jersey, for tennis greats like Bobby Riggs and Jack Kramer.

In the summer of 1941, at age 14, Dick won a local junior tournament in Maplewood, New Jersey. Three years later, his family moved to El Paso, Texas, because of his mother's health.

At El Paso High School he was a second-team All American choice in basketball as well as Texas state tennis champion. In 1946, Savitt entered Cornell University but during his first year he injured his knee and was forced to concentrate on tennis. In 1947 and 1948 he was ranked twenty-sixth in the country in tennis.

In 1949 Savitt, 6 foot 3 and weighing 185 pounds, won the Eastern Intercollegiate Tennis Tournament held in Syracuse, New York, and was ranked sixteenth nationally. In 1950, ranked sixth in the country, he reached the semifinals of the U.S. Nationals at Forest Hills. He won several other tournaments.

He combined a powerful serve with deep, hard-hit ground strokes that forced opponents to remain in the backcourt on the defensive.

In January 1951 he won the Australian Open. In July he took the men's singles at Wimbledon, defeating Herb Flam in the semifinals and Ken MacGregor in the finals. *The New York Times* called Savitt the "world's number one amateur player." *Time* magazine wrote a cover story on August 27, 1951, about his impressive playing. He was the only Jew ever to win a Wimbledon singles title.

Between 1950 and 1952, Savitt was ranked in the top

Dick Savitt, the 1951 Wimbledon Singles Champion (far left), teaching tennis in Israel.

Israel Tennis Center

ten. When Savitt and Herb Flam made the Davis Cup squad in 1951, it marked the first time that Jewish players were included on the team.

In October 1952 Savitt announced his retirement from big-time competitive tennis in order, as he put it then, "to go to work." Unlike today, in the early 1950s top-ranked tennis players earned very little money.

For thirty years, Savitt worked as a stockbroker in New York, and since 1979 he has directed the Israel Tennis Center's program which teaches coaches how to instruct. He visits Israel twice a year and works with Israeli players when they visit the United States.

Winning Wimbledon was not Dick's greatest moment in tennis. Capturing the National Father and Son Championships in 1981 with his son, Robert, was.

Dick Savitt is a member of the Jewish Sports Hall of Fame in Israel.

Dolph Schayes

Basketball's First Modern Forward

Dolph Schayes, 6 feet 8 inches tall, was hardly a giant by basketball standards, yet he was a towering figure on the basketball court when he played for the NBA's Syracuse Nationals in the 1950s and early 1960s. He was considered the first modern basketball forward: big, fast, mobile.

Dolph was born in 1928 in New York City. He inherited both his love for sports and his height from his father, a Romanian Jew who was an avid sports fan and 6 feet 4 inches tall. Playing sandlot football as a youngster, Dolph once carried the ball through the line. A guard grabbed one leg, a tackle, the other. One of them said, "Let's make a wish." It was then that Dolph decided to switch to basketball for good!

Though Dolph was an All-American basketball player at New York University, Dolph's coach thought that he lacked the physique to make it as a pro. But Syracuse took him on, switching him from center to forward.

He was named Rookie of the Year in 1949. His two-handed set shots and driving lay-ups were nearly unstoppable and his foul-shooting was excellent. His record for the most free throws made (6,979) stood until 1972. Each time Dolph scored a basket he ran to the opposite end of the court, his fist clenched triumphantly above his head.

He played in 764 straight games, including playoffs, between February 17, 1952 and December 27, 1961. Once in 1952, he broke his right wrist and, while it was in a cast, continued to play.

In 1951 he won the rebounding title, and at his retirement in 1963 he was fourth on the all-time rebounding list. In 1957 Dolph broke Minneapolis Laker George Mikan's career point total of 11,764. Schayes won the NBA

Most Valuable Player Award five times.

With Schayes, the Nats won only one world championship (in 1955) but always made the playoffs. When Dolph retired, he had scored more points (19,249) than any other player in the game.

In 1964, when the Nats left Syracuse to become the Philadelphia 76ers, Dolph became their head coach. He was named NBA Coach of the Year for leading the 76ers to the NBA title during the 1965-66 season. He was fired the next year after his team failed to retain the title. From 1966 to 1970 Dolph served as supervisor of NBA referees.

Schayes felt that being Jewish had little or no effect on his basketball career. "There was never any hint of anti-Semitism in pro basketball," he said. "Since many of the fans in the large metropolitan area were Jewish in the early days of the NBA, I was fairly well received." He is a member of the Basketball Hall of Fame and the Jewish Sports Hall of Fame in Israel.

His son Danny Schayes is presently a star center for the Milwaukee Bucks in the NBA. Dolph did not insist that Danny take up the game. But, after learning the fundamentals from his father at home, "it was hard not to enjoy the game," Danny recalled.

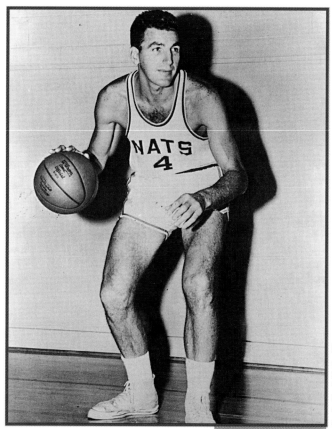

Basketball Hall of Fame

Dolph Schayes: Superstar in the NBA during the 1950s.

Mathieu Schneider

Ice Hockey Star for the Montreal Canadiens

When Mathieu Schneider was three years old, his father Sam bought him a pair of ice skates and took him to the Rockefeller Center ice skating rink in New York City so he could try them out.

Encouraged by his father, Mathieu took up ice hockey as a youngster. He followed his father's advice and played defense. "It's more of a thinking position than playing wing," said Mathieu. "You get to see a whole play develop in front of you."

Mathieu is small for hockey, weighing "only" 190 pounds. He tries to make up for that by being aggressive on the ice. Unimpressed with the way hockey was taught in New Jersey, where Mathieu lived, his father began a hockey school with his two sons, Mathieu and Jean Alain, as pupils.

Moving to Rhode Island when he was 12, Mathieu attended a Catholic school, Mount Saint-Charles Academy.

Mathieu left Mount Saint-Charles Academy after the 11th grade and, at age 17, began playing for the Cornwall Royals of the Ontario Junior Hockey League. He scored 36 points in 63 games.

After his first season with the Royals he was drafted by the Montreal Canadiens. It was, said Mathieu, "a dream come true." After a four-game tryout with the Canadiens, Mathieu joined the Sherbrooke Canadiens, an American Hockey League team that belongs to the Montreal Canadiens organization.

After a strong 1989 season with Sherbrooke, Schneider was called up to play for the Canadiens. As a National Hockey League (NHL) rookie, he exhibited solid offensive and defensive skills.

On September 7, 1991, Mathieu signed a three-year

contract with the Montreal Canadiens. In the spring of 1991, during a game between the Canadiens and the Buffalo Sabres, one of the Sabres uttered some abusive words at Schneider, using the word "Jew" derisively. Schneider patiently waited for the right opportunity, then ran the fellow into the sideboards. The incident made the newspapers. "I'm sure a lot more people realized I am Jewish through that," said Schneider.

Mathieu's French-Canadian mother Aline converted from Catholicism to Judaism when she married Mathieu's father. "I am a proud Jew, and I will bring up my kids to be proud Jews," Schneider said emphatically.

Montreal Canadiens

Mathieu Schneider: Montreal Canadiens pro hockey star, shows off his defensive skills on the ice.

Mark Spitz

Greatest Swimmer in History

Mark Spitz has been called the greatest Jewish athlete of all time. Many consider him the best of all swimmers as well.

Born in Modesto, California, in 1950, Mark learned to swim at age six. Two years later he was practicing swimming 75 minutes a day. He thought little of becoming a swimming star; he wanted to be someone like (pro football star quarterback) Johnny Unitas.

The Spitz family moved from Sacramento to Santa Clara so that Mark could attend George Haines' successful Santa Clara (California) Swim Club there.

At age 10, Mark's swimming lessons interfered with his Hebrew school. Swimming took priority. Mark's father, rationalizing his son's absence from Hebrew school, insisted that "even God likes a winner."

In 1965, at age 15, Mark won four gold medals and set four new records at the Maccabiah Games in Israel. Getting all those firsts "did something for me," he said. Mark's first outstanding year occurred in 1967 when he set five American and seven world records in the 100- and 200-meter butterfly races and the 400-meter freestyle. *Swimming World* magazine called him "World Swimmer of the Year."

At the American trials for the 1968 Olympics in Mexico City, Spitz confidently predicted that he would outswim everyone. While he won two gold medals in the relays, a silver in the 10-meter butterfly, and a bronze in the 100-meter freestyle, he finished last in the final of the 200-meter butterfly. His three attempts at a gold medal in an individual event had failed.

He won six swimming gold medals at the 1969 Maccabiah Games and was named the Games' outstanding athlete. In 1971 Mark became the first Jewish recipient of the American Athletic Union's James E. Sullivan Award, given to the amateur athlete of the year.

Mark carried his 170 pounds on a tightly compact 6 foot, 1 inch frame. He was able to flex his lower legs slightly forward at the knees, which enabled him to kick six to 12 inches deeper into water than his opponents.

At Munich, in 1972, Spitz gave the greatest swimming exhibition ever recorded. He won seven gold medals: four for individual events (the 100- and 200-meter freestyle and the 100- and 200-meter butterfly) and three for the relays; all were in world record time.

His attempt to make a comeback at the age of 41 in 1992 was highly publicized but proved a failure.

Mark once said: "I feel that being a Jewish athlete has helped our cause. We have shown that we are as good as the next guy."

Zvi Nishri, Physical Education and Sport Archives of the Wingate Institute of Physical Education and Sport, Netanya, Israel

Mark Spitz holds torch at the opening of the 12th Maccabiah Games in 1985.

Steve Stone

1980 Cy Young Award Winner

Pitching for the Baltimore Orioles, Steve Stone won 25 games and lost seven in 1980. The performance earned him the Cy Young Award as the best pitcher in the American League.

Born in Cleveland, Ohio, in 1947, Steve was an all-around athlete as a youngster. He shot a hole in one at golf at age 11 and, at age 13, won the Cleveland junior tennis title.

His father fixed jukeboxes; his mother was a waitress. Steve won All-State honors in baseball as a junior at Bush High School in Cleveland from where he was graduated in 1965. His idol was Dodger pitcher Sandy Koufax.

Stone graduated from Kent State University in Kent, Ohio, in 1969, with a degree in history and government, and because of a distinguished baseball record at Kent, he signed with the San Francisco Giants on February 15, 1969.

First, he pitched for two years in the minor leagues; then, in 1971 he pitched for the San Francisco Giants before being traded to the Chicago White Sox in 1973. A year later he was traded to the Chicago Cubs. In 1975 he was 12-8 for the Cubs.

A sore shoulder almost forced him to quit baseball in 1976, but he recovered and had a good season with the White Sox. In 1977 Stone achieved a career high of 15 wins (15-12) with the White Sox. In 1978 he signed to play with the Baltimore Orioles. Steve had a bonus provision in his contract whereby he would receive an extra $100,000 in any season that he won the Cy Young Award. "It was like an insurance salesman telling you, 'We'll give you $50,000 if an elephant falls on your head.' He knows darn well an elephant isn't going to fall on you.'"

Well, an elephant fell on Steve Stone in 1980. He was

2-3 with a 4.74 earned run average through early May. But he won the next 23 of 27 games that he pitched with a 3.06 earned run average. He had 14 straight wins at one point. Steve Stone's 25 wins led the majors that year.

Steve credited his improved win record to pitching faster so that the fielders would stay alert between pitches. He was also able to find his best pitch—usually his curve—in the early innings and stick with it.

When asked how his fellow players reacted to the fact that he is Jewish, he said, "I've always been proud of being Jewish. If you're a good enough pitcher, they don't care if you're a Martian."

After retiring as a player, he did the television play by play of the Chicago Cubs games.

Baltimore Orioles

Ready to fire a strike: pitcher Steve Stone, the 1980 Cy Young Award Winner.

INDEX